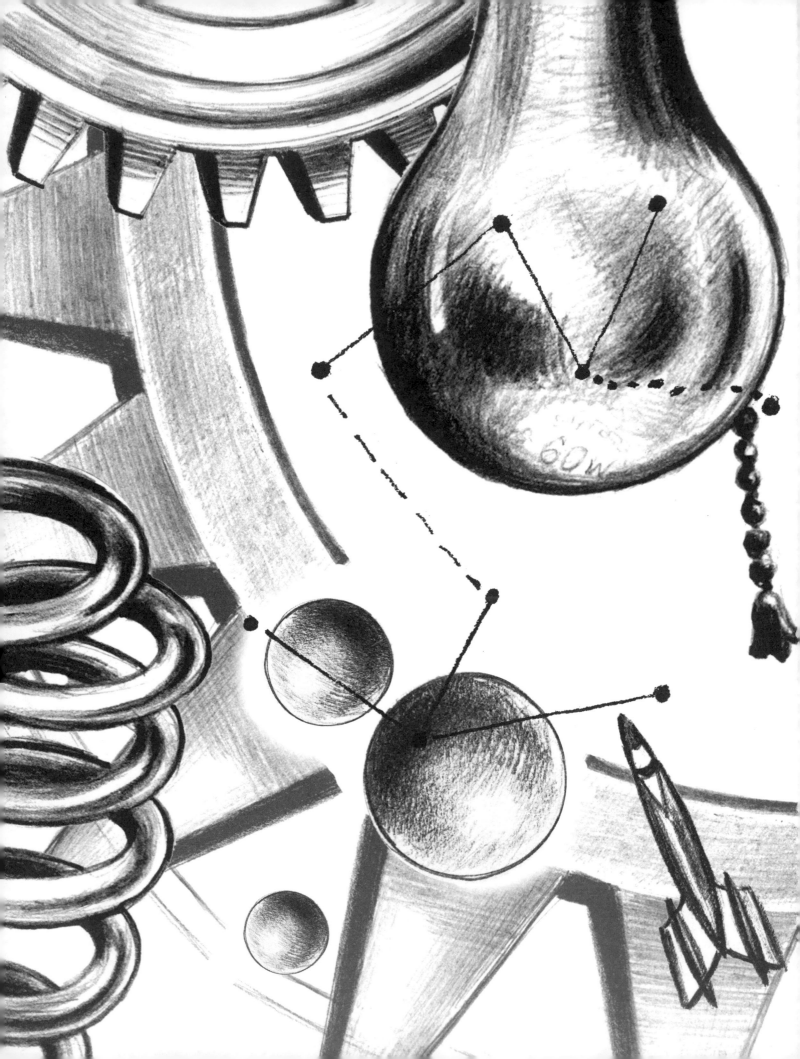

It's Cool To Be Clever

The story of Edson C. Hendricks,
the genius who invented the design
for the INTERNET

LEANNE JONES
Illustrated by Anna Mah

Agio
PUBLISHING HOUSE

This book is dedicated to
Kali, Alice, Farrah, Zuzu and Florence,
and to children everywhere.

PUBLISHING HOUSE

151 Howe Street, Victoria BC Canada V8V 4K5

For rights information and bulk orders, please contact
info@agiopublishing.com or go to www.agiopublishing.com

It's Cool To Be Clever
ISBN 978-1-897435-63-2 (hardbound edition)
ISBN 978-1-897435-64-9 (eBook edition)

Cataloguing information available from Library and Archives Canada.

Printed in Canada on acid-free paper.
Manufactured by Friesens Corporation in Altona, MB, Canada,
May 2011, Job # 65055.

Agio Publishing House is a socially responsible company, measuring
success on a triple-bottom-line basis.

10   9   8   7   6   5   4   3   2   1

Have you ever wondered how the Internet was really invented? Well, I would like to tell you. My name is Edson Hendricks, and I know because I am the one who invented the network design upon which the Internet is based.

I was born on May 22nd, 1945, and raised in the small town of Lemoyne, Pennsylvania, right across the Susquehanna River from Harrisburg, the state capital. Almost all the people who lived in Lemoyne and neighboring towns were white, middle class, Protestant Christians. Most folks had very fixed ideas about religion, race, and how everyone "should" be. It made people a bit uneasy if a young boy asked too many questions or was inventive.

By the time I started grade school in September of 1951, I felt quite cool, because I already knew how to read! Every Sunday my father held my sister, Willa, and me on his knee and read the comics to us. I loved the comic strip characters Little Lulu and Nancy and Sluggo, who were always inventing new ways to have fun and often got into trouble. While my father read, it was so pleasant that I followed along with the words, and before long I could read by myself.

The thing I disliked on Sundays was always having to go to church. Already I was becoming very independent, and inclined to rebel against constraints imposed by organized society and fixed systems. My feeling is that there is always room for improvement, and constraints stifle creativity.

At Washington Heights Elementary School, the principal was Mrs. Gardner, who was also the sixth grade teacher. I had some friends in grade school like anyone else, but there was a little problem with the fact that my father was the principal of the high school right next door, and I had bright red hair.

There was a group of boys who made me feel pretty sensitive about my hair.

"Carrot-top! Carrot-top!" they teased.

I always replied, "That's silly. Carrot tops are green." But the taunting made me uneasy. I wanted to be invisible.

My favorite subjects were math and science, and I got the top marks. Yet when I proudly wrote a column about those topics for the school's monthly newsletter, Mrs. Gardner dampened my enthusiasm.

"Perhaps you should write the column without signing your name, in view of your father's role in our school system," Mrs. Gardner suggested. "People might think he wrote it for you."

That suited me just fine, and I began to enjoy being anonymous.

I felt like I was walking on egg shells because of my father's status in the community and the boys' taunting. So what did I do about it, you might ask?

Having the big imagination that I have, I created an imaginary world. In this world I was a machine made up of mechanical components instead of biological internal organs. This world was great because machines do not feel sad or need connections like people. And that was when I found I liked and understood machines better than humans!

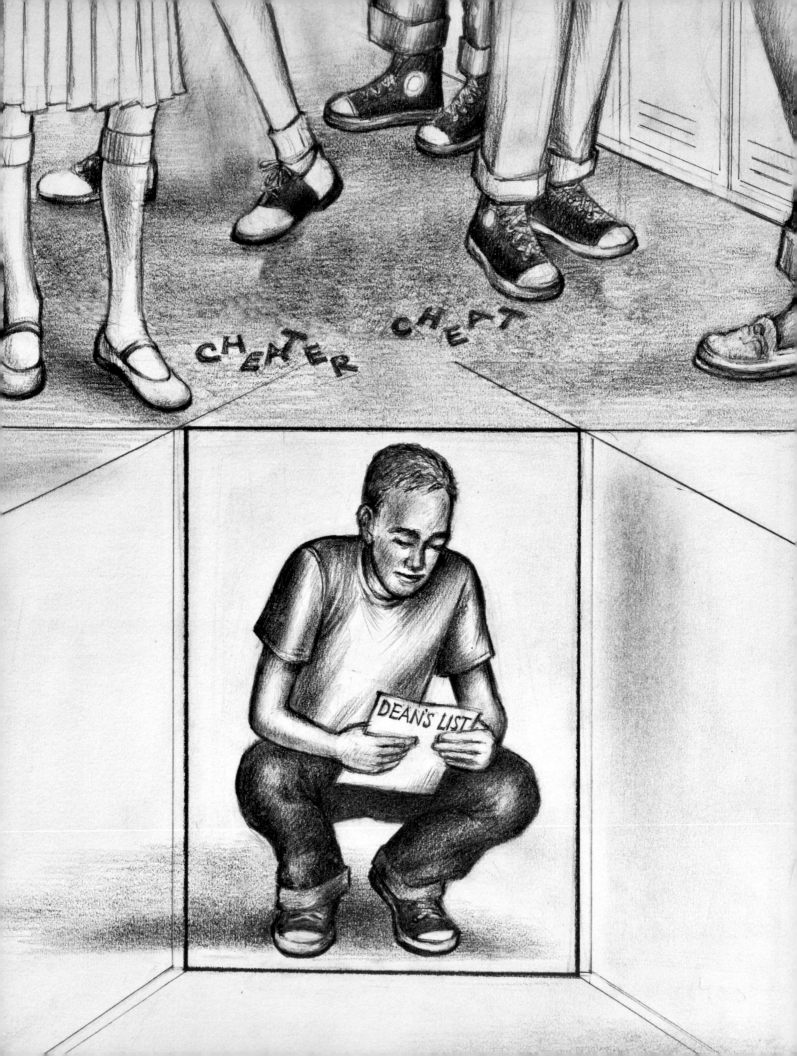

In high school, I became quite aware of the dangers of my own impulsiveness to experiment. One day one of my backyard experiments generated a really big explosion that rocked our whole house. My parents came rushing out to see what had happened.

"What was that!?" my father asked in a loud, worried voice.

"Oh, nothing," I told him. "Just a minor *misestimate*."

Really, it was a nightmare being the son of the principal. My marks were exemplary but the other kids thought I must be getting secret help from my father.

"Edson gets his answers for the tests from you-know-who," I could hear the other students whispering, loud enough for me to hear.

One of the parents, Mrs. Johnson, whose son was not doing well academically, said, "And what would you expect, from someone whose father is the principal?"

As a child I wasn't very excited about sports, but I neither liked nor hated them. In late grade school I did try out for the Little League baseball team, but it wasn't for me. It was too boring waiting to catch fly balls, especially when I'd rather be grabbing onto new ideas. Only later, as an adult in Boston, did I come to understand baseball and enjoy watching it.

I started to feel sad when I entered high school. Before starting grade school, I thought it was rather cool to be clever, but I gradually found out that the other kids were jealous and their taunting got worse in the higher grades. I had pretty much gotten past my imaginary machine world and was now face-to-face with reality.

My mother told me she hated my situation and tried to get my father to agree to send me somewhere else to school, but he wouldn't have it. He wanted me to go to his school. That was so cruel of him, I thought at the time. I felt misunderstood and knew right then, I was different right down to the color of my hair.

Gathering up my courage in grade nine, I joined the football team and did pretty well at that. In one game I pretty much single-handedly saved the game by running very fast and tackling a player from the other team who was sprinting toward our goal line. If he'd gotten that touchdown, they would have won. For a few days after that, I felt maybe I could fit in with the other students better. But the feeling didn't last.

I dropped football when I got into tenth grade. I just didn't like playing football very much. Too many people and too much emotional up and down.

lthough I was in high school and more realistic, I was no less interested in machines. By this time, I was enjoying my privacy and was actively looking for mental challenge and adventure toward making new things work better. I read every technical magazine I could get my hands on at the local library, such as *Popular Science, Scientific American, Popular Mechanics* and *Mechanix Illustrated*.

I was a very active problem solver. When the first transistor radios appeared, I picked one up right away, then set to work figuring out how it worked inside. Soon I was building my own radios.

One day I saw a man servicing a pinball machine. He had the front of the machine opened up so all the workings were exposed. I examined the insides of it, all loaded up with mechanical relays used to control its operation. I could just see it was very old technology.

I suggested to the service man that all those mechanical switches should be replaced with the new semiconductor logic, as it would be a lot cheaper, more reliable, smaller, more power-efficient and so on.

"Get lost, kid, and stop bothering me," the guy said.

About ten years later pinball machine makers did exactly what I had suggested to him.

In my teens, when I learned that the Massachusetts Institute of Technology, or MIT for short, was the very best college for math and science, I wanted to go there.

"That school is attended by the very best brains in the entire nation and from other countries, too. Don't you know that?" asked my father. My parents thought it was unrealistic, so I decided to show them. I studied extra hard, with a clear goal in mind.

Everyone was very surprised when I was accepted by MIT. Except me, because I knew I was as clever as anyone else.

In September of 1963, I went to Cambridge, which is near Boston in Massachusetts, and entered MIT as a freshman. When I made the Dean's List for very high grades that first year, I felt elated by this sweet success. MIT wrote letters to my family and my high school to congratulate them. So my parents, teachers and friends at my old school as well as anyone who doubted my ability, were now ready to admit that I was, well, pretty clever, and maybe even a bit cool.

I was proud to be on the Dean's List every year while at MIT.

One day at MIT I realized that I needed money as well as brains, so I visited the student employment center and found out that they could offer me one of two jobs. The first one was washing light bulbs. The other was the one I took, which was operating the huge new International Business Machines (IBM) System 360 model 65 computer.

Back then, there were no personal computers as we know them today -- only massive "mainframe" computers at the largest universities, government agencies and businesses. Mainframe computers were used as scientific and business calculators, and had no capability for sharing music, emailing, watching video or playing games. In fact, a mainframe computer couldn't easily connect to any other computers – that would come much later.

The IBM 360/65 was in a huge, secured, air conditioned room of its own. There was one big metal box about the size of a small school bus in the center of the room, which was the central processing unit (we called it the CPU) and all of the magnetic core memory. All around it were various other connected pieces, which resembled lines of refrigerators. Some of these, probably a dozen, were huge tape decks, others were disk storage units and other controllers. Instructions were entered on a typewriter and on paper cards with tiny rectangular holes in a pattern. The results of computations were printed out on accordion-folded continuous streams of paper.

The first night on the job, after a three-minute introduction, I was left alone in the computer room.

"What a load of fun," I thought to myself, and then I had one of the most wonderful evenings of my life, working all those dials and things for which I had an instinctive aptitude.

In the following weeks, I overheard the boss saying, "That

Edson is a really cool clever kid on those machines. Let's put him straight into the job of system programmer." And that's what they did.

A system programmer is the one who makes computers work. Maybe my early imaginings and empathy with machines helped me understand them better. It wasn't long before I heard comments like, "Edson Hendricks is the most expert system programmer in the whole Boston area."

The 360/65 was a quite new product and we were pushing it to its capacity. IBM workers started coming to me to learn how to run and fix their own company's computer products. It felt good to be appreciated for being clever. No one cared if my hair was red, and no one knew what my father's job was.

MIT professor J.C.R. Licklider envisioned linking computers together in a network. But an idea needs work to really happen. He and Dr. Larry Roberts convinced the US military's Advanced Research Projects Agency, or ARPA, to hire a team of computer scientists who worked for many years on what would become known as the ARPANET. After they got ARPANET working in late 1969, a few dozen mainframe computers were connected over the next four years. ARPANET was not available to the public and it was very costly to operate and didn't connect many computers, but it was a start.

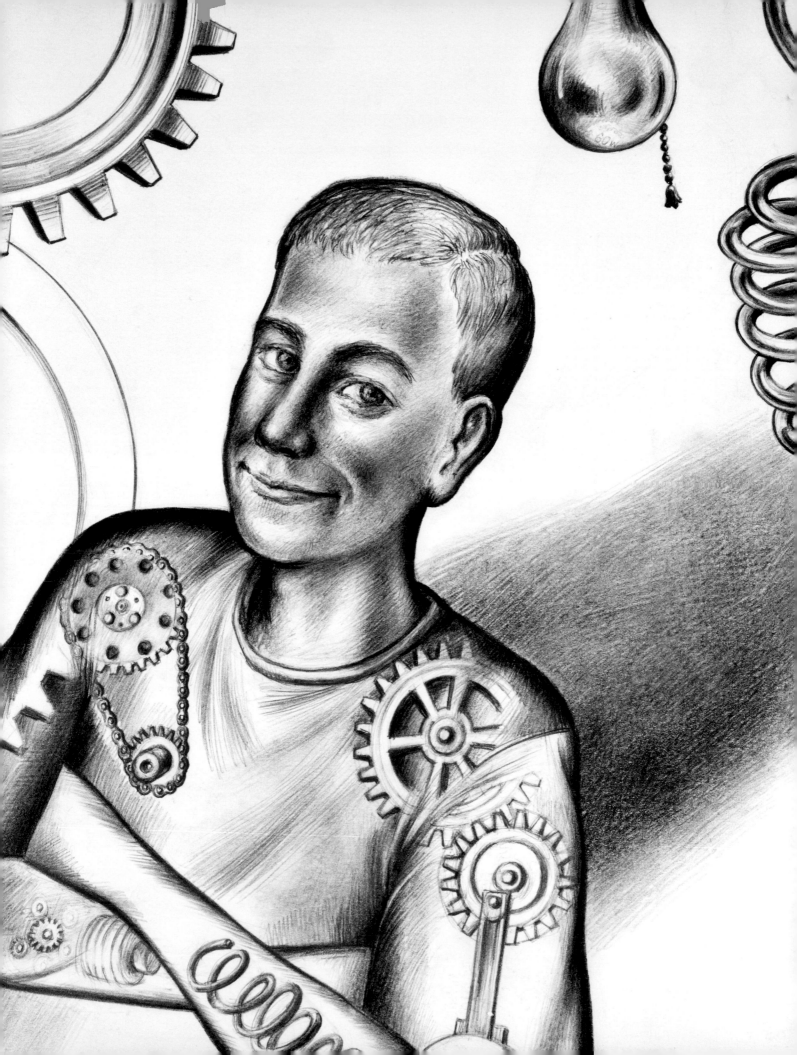

When I first started to work as a system programmer on the IBM 360/65 mainframe computer, there was no video display – what today we'd call a computer screen or monitor. Results from the computer were printed out on paper. So it was pretty exciting when we installed the new IBM 2250 Model 1 video display.

In my spare time, I created a little game project with the new video display, just to learn how to work it. This was around 1965, and what was probably the first computer video game in the world had been created one floor up in the same building by MIT student Steve Russell using a DEC PDP-1 computer. Both his game and mine were called *Spacewar*.

There was a sun in the center with gravity and two rocket ships. Talented players could get their rockets orbiting around the sun. The ships could be aimed and accelerated; when accelerating each ship would emit an animated rocket exhaust. The ships could shoot missiles at each other. The missiles were also drawn by the sun's gravity, so a missile's path would curve depending on how close to the sun it was. *Spacewar* was pretty primitive, but it was, after all, the first computer video game ever running on an IBM 360, and probably the first one in the world ever to be seen (and played) by the general public.

Here's what happened. Each year, MIT had an Open House weekend so people interested in MIT could look over the Institute. *Spacewar* was set up as a display in the computer area. Really, nobody regularly there at MIT thought the game was anything extraordinary, including myself.

Soon enough the parents noticed, and throughout Open House weekend they went to the

Computation Center to leave their kids while the parents looked over the rest of the campus. There would be kids stacked eight or nine deep trying to get to play a game they'd never seen before, nor heard of.

At one point, an argument broke out. "It's my turn," said a tall lanky kid.

"You already had one," said a smaller younger one.

"You wanna make something of it?"

"I sure do," said the other kid.

And before I knew it, I was settling what was possibly the world's first fight about a video game. I couldn't quite get my mind around the fact that this game was that popular.

Right after the weekend, the MIT management insisted that I remove my game because they thought it was wasting too much expensive computer time. Amusingly, each year when the Open House weekend came, they asked me to bring it back.

Then a mysterious incident occurred. One night, someone broke into my office. My office door was locked, but the burglar was able to get in by scaling up the outside hall wall about ten feet to open a window and climb into my office. Then he dug through my files to find my copy of the *Spacewar* game.

Apparently some of the staff at MIT had started playing the game, but were frustrated when it was removed from the big computer. Following a trail of clues, I tracked down the culprit. It was a fellow student who quickly confessed. "I'm sorry," he said. "I had a strong feeling that I *had* to have it."

We both thought that it was pretty funny, actually! Who knew that computer games could be so addictive? He and I became friends.

In June 1967, I graduated with a Bachelor's Degree in Electrical Engineering and began graduate studies with Professor Licklider. Soon I became aware of some ground-breaking computer work being done just across the street at the IBM Cambridge Scientific Center. I began hanging out there.

One day, I decided I'd just ask the IBM people if they'd like me to work there. They said definitely, they'd already copied a bunch of my own original programming code. So I left MIT graduate school and went to work for IBM in March 1968. I've never regretted that at all. It was my very best choice because I wanted to invent.

My new managers asked me to develop a network – a way for computers to connect together to exchange information – between IBM's scientific centers. They expected me to copy the latest ARPANET design. I looked carefully at ARPANET for a very long time sitting in my office. Their network was too expensive, needing dedicated cabling between all the computer centers, and extra computers to manage the transmissions. *There had to be something simpler – a design that could simply and cheaply connect all types of computers all around the world.*

The Scientific Center was a very special place conjured up by its founder and manager Norman Rasmussen. Inventing takes a great deal of thinking, technical know-how and creativity which Norman thought could only happen if the creative process could be protected from other business pressures. So I was left undisturbed to work on my assignment. In fact, I spent *almost two years* mostly just staring at a wall, thinking. And then it all began to happen….

Knowing machines as I did, I realized that machines do not need connections like people do talking on telephones. Making a phone call, one had to dial a number for another telephone, and the system would establish a continuous connection between the two telephones for the duration of the conversation. The reason for this telephone network design is that when two people are conversing, timing is *very* important. A long pause or a quick reply mean different things in people's conversation. But not when computers communicate! When a computer had something to send to another computer, it could just send it without needing to establish any connection first, or to wait for an immediate reply. So that was my big discovery: that unlike the timing in people's conversations, the timing in machine communication is less important. Removing the need for fixed connections would allow a network to expand to connect all the computers in the world without the added cost for dedicated lines.

By 1973, I had the earliest, most rudimentary version of my design working on several computers.

To my amazement, and everyone else's, the network just took off, with people eager to add in their computer. I knew machines, but this was far beyond my own expectations. The network actually started organizing itself! I called it VNET, short for virtual network. It quickly became the unofficial internal IBM computer

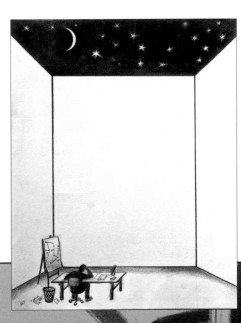

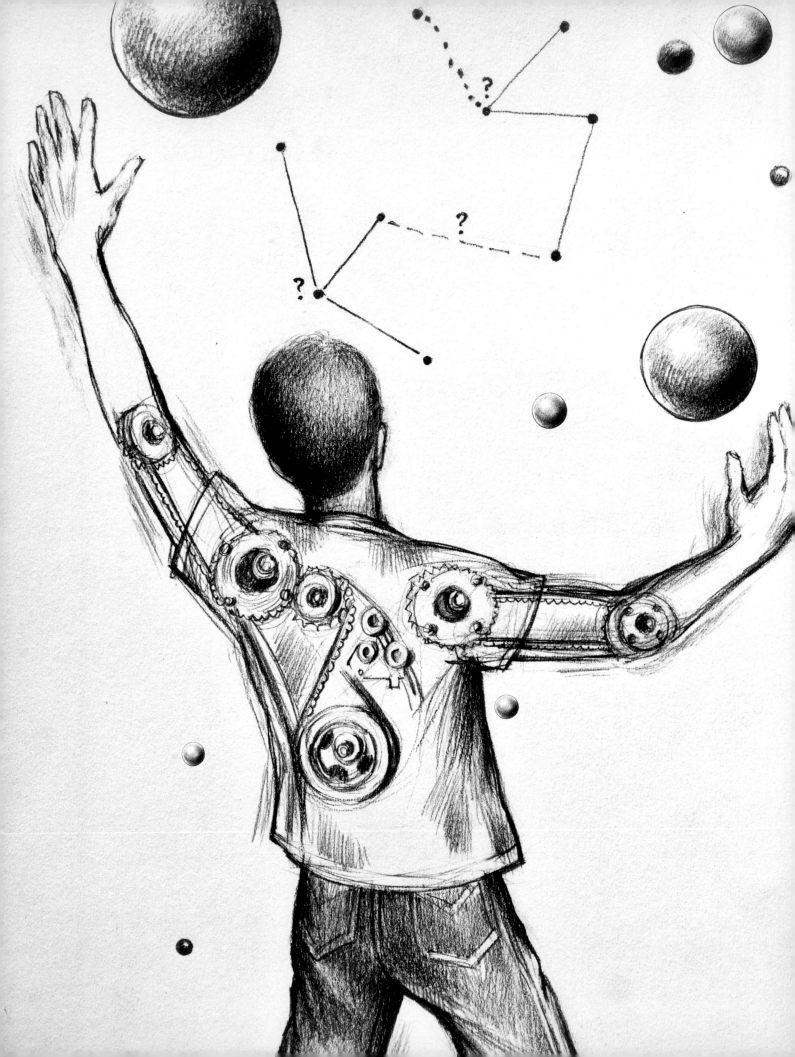

network, connecting hundreds of big mainframe computers around the world. This network was used by everyone in IBM who used computers, to send and exchange electronic mail and other data.

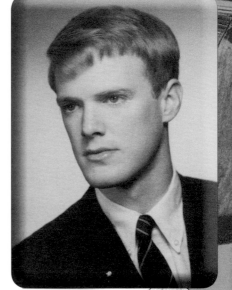

VNET was the world's first widely adopted "connectionless" network. Over the next decade, people in universities around the world became aware of VNET and created their own similar networks, based on my VNET software. In Europe it was called EARN; in Canada, there was NETNORTH; and in the USA, universities created BITNET and USENET/UUNET. The design would spread in many other ways and places, simply because VNET's approach worked so efficiently.

But back in the mid-1970s, the IBM top bosses could not envision the implications of my invention, even though VNET was fully operational and already making a great deal of money for IBM through licensing and streamlining our worldwide communications. The bosses wanted to *control* all computer users' communications through a single network they had commissioned, called Systems Network Architecture or SNA. But SNA didn't really work yet and users didn't want IBM to control their communications. When my invention was presented as an alternative to SNA, it was clear that the bosses were committed to their SNA, so a great business opportunity was lost for IBM. I was ordered to stop developing VNET.

So I became very frustrated and somewhat depressed, and that was when I had the feeling of giving up because the very hardest part, when it comes to inventions, is changing people's way of thinking.

My friend Chet noticed how sad and depressed I was, so he suggested a sailing trip. He and I set out to sea on the way from Boston to Bermuda in June of 1975.

"Buck up, man," said Chet. "Let's try and enjoy this voyage. That's the whole idea."

Once we were well out on the sea, Chet yelled, "Look over there!"

It was a school of leaping, frolicking whales! I have to admit it was beautiful to see the sight of baby whales at play. We watched them roll and sparkle in the sun. Suddenly, the enormous mother whale made her appearance beside us. Chet and I kept very quiet, calm and not speaking, simply trying hard to blend into the surroundings as the group passed very, very close to our small sailboat.

We pushed on and on for several days, until our wind just died. For 7 days and 7 nights we were without wind and couldn't do anything so we played cards, talked and enjoyed the perfect peace of the moment. Then suddenly we were visited by a US Navy ship. It came up to us and stopped nearby, so we had to start our outboard motor to go over next to them.

There was an awkward silence when we got there, which Chet broke by yelling up to the 100 or so sailors aboard who were staring down at us, "What are you guys doing out here!?"

They all laughed, since it was meant to be a joke, of course.

The captain asked us if we were all right and if we knew where we were. We replied that we were fine. He gave us our exact position, which was just what we thought. And he asked us if we knew we were being carried out toward the middle of the Atlantic Ocean by the Gulf Stream current. We replied that

we did, and we didn't like it, but there was nothing we could do until we got some wind.

So the Navy ship left, and several days later an intense storm formed right on top of us, without any warning at all. We had no way to avoid it. Before this fierce gale I was so deeply sad that I really had thoughts of giving up on life completely, but suddenly we were in the fight of our lives. The waves were so powerful and Chet seemed to lose his resolve. Luckily, he had on board a book called *How to Sail in a Hurricane* which told us we had to sail into the wind. The winds and waves were frighteningly strong, but we fought and fought to keep the boat's bow pointed into the wind.

Although we had been reported missing, in the end we finally managed to get to our destination, Bermuda.

On our arrival in Bermuda, officials who interviewed us were surprised to hear our description of the ocean suddenly turning all white with thick foam. They explained its significance to us. This was a clear sign that the winds reached hurricane strength where we were.

Looking back, I think sailing through a hurricane was the best test of my character because, although I still felt very sad, I also felt more determined to get back to the fight of having my invention accepted and widely adopted.

I thought, since I survived a hurricane at sea in a small sailboat and learned a whole lot in the process, I really should try again.

If I'd died either due to myself or the weather, who would have pushed for the development of today's Internet? I could really see the advantage of a computer network being completely linked around the world. I wondered if my VNET and ARPANET could be a good fit together.

Soon after it got back to Cambridge, my friend, MIT professor Jerry Saltzer, said to me, "Edson, your idea is just too good to stay hidden. We are going to Washington, my friend." So that is just what we did.

Jerry and I flew to Washington, DC, to visit ARPA to explain the design behind VNET.

We arrived at Washington National Airport and rented a car. Jerry was in the front passenger seat, and I was driving. Jerry told me he knew roughly where ARPA was, but he wasn't sure of its exact location. So I asked Jerry if he would recognize the building if he saw it, and he told me he definitely would.

Then I suggested to him I'd just keep driving around trying to avoid retracing my more-or-less random route. He should keep

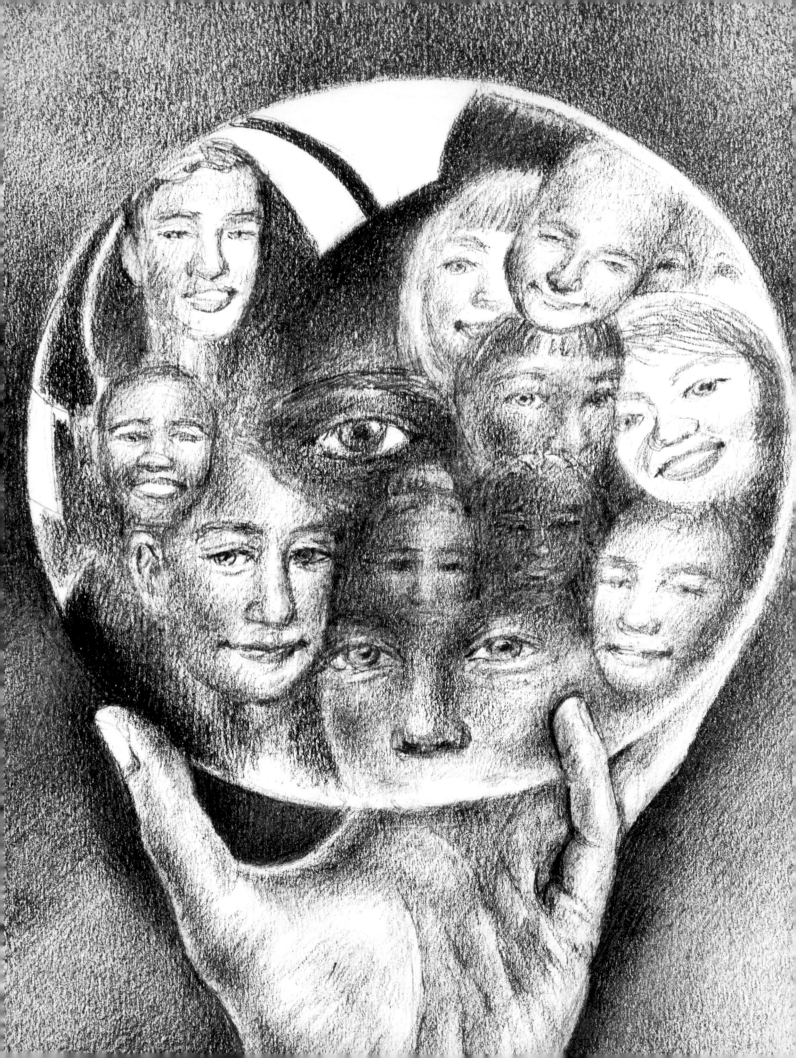

a sharp watch out the window, and when he saw ARPA, give a shout. So we did that. After several minutes, Jerry spotted ARPA and gave his shout. And I told him, that's how to do simple and effective message routing in a computer network! The packets of information keep traveling all around the network until the intended destination is reached. The information would find the recipient at the speed of electricity, even though there was no direct, fixed, one-to-one connection.

When we got to ARPA and made our presentation, the principal scientist, Dr. Vinton G. Cerf, told me, "Edson, I really like what you've done. Now perhaps we can advance your idea."

From that point on, Vint and other ARPA scientists, and their colleagues in companies and at universities around the world, began to change ARPANET to become connectionless. Many of those scientists had experienced using VNET already. The result developed into the Internet we know today.

I was delighted when they designed a protocol, which is a rule about how data moves from one place to another, similar to my VNET design. Strangely, they left out some rules from my design, including instant messaging, which had to be added decades later. Today people do that on their cell phones, calling it *text messaging* or simply *texting*.

And so the Internet took on a life of its own -- growing just like my earlier network called VNET had before -- as can be seen by the impact of computer networking in today's life. Those connections and central controls that previously prevented machines from exchanging data efficiently are proof that often the greatest things in life are free. That's what I had seen after staring for months at the wall: the world's first "connectionless" computer network for everyone, with no one company or government controlling it, and people around the world able to join freely.

Sometimes I do feel weird because people in most countries on Earth are using the Internet system that I originally devised. And who knows? Maybe one day the Internet will even save the world, because it has given a voice to the common people everywhere. Now they can speak freely with everyone in the world.

The magical world of inventing entails the ability to observe *very* well, come up with ideas, then try them out. A few years ago, when I went to visit my sister in Philadelphia, we visited her friend and I met their amazing cat named Smedley. He was an Abyssinian, a breed of cat that is smart, very independent, yet very attached to any person it likes.

I immediately had an affinity for Smedley. Finally I'd met a character like myself and it turned out to be a cat! He brought out my observational ability. As we entered each room, there was Smedley, sitting right at the door grinning at us, even though I couldn't catch him going past us anywhere in the hall. I could tell he just loved this game he'd created.

Back in the living room, Smedley began entertaining us with his act of sitting perfectly still in a doorway, and then suddenly leaping straight up, landing perfectly on the half-inch molding edge above the doorway and standing there, grinning back down at us. He did that several times, seemingly defying gravity, just to prove it wasn't a fluke. Amazing!

Next, Smedley went over and sat next to a closet, staring back at his owner. She went over, opened the closet, and pulled out a large mailing tube. Smedley was instantly very excited.

The mailing tube was made of heavy cardboard, about three feet long, maybe about four inches in diameter, sealed at one end and open at the other. The owner rolled the mailing tube out on the floor. Before it stopped rolling, Smedley dove straight into the open end and disappeared.

How in the world, I wondered, will this cat back out of the mailing tube? It wasn't nearly big enough for a cat of Smedley's size to turn around in. I wondered if a cat could actually back out. After about half a minute of suspense, Smedley came out of the tube head first!

"Now whaat? How did he do that?"

My best guess is that the cat had a magician's cleverness. He was smart enough to exploit the confusion surrounding the rolling out of the mailing tube in the first place to make it look as if he had gone in head first, but what he had actually done was to back into it. If that's what happened, then that was one really darn good cat magician.

Soon the conversation moved to going out for dinner. The second Smedley heard such talk, he stalked straight over to the door and planted himself in front of it to block anyone from leaving. This clever cat evidently could understand some English. To get Smedley out of the way, the owner had to pick him up, stroke him and talk gently. "We are just going out for a while," she said soothingly, "and we will all be back soon enough."

Smedley grudgingly gave in and walked away a little, but still stayed close.

I was impressed with Smedley, who could observe his situation *very* closely, consider his options and invent new behaviors. He set a great example: If he can invent, surely you can too!

I am nearing the end of my story, and I would like to encourage you now. If you have some really interesting ideas, don't be afraid to talk about them or to pursue them. Make good observations and then capture them in your mind and on paper. Observations don't need to be just about facts and technical data – they can be found in the magic of daily life, by staring at a blank wall, the sky, or even a clever cat. Allow your imagination to flow out, because from those ideas come other ideas. But be prepared to work very hard to convince others that you have a very important idea.

Sometimes an idea may seem impossible. Before I took a crack at creating a network like the Internet, the common thinking was that it would be impossible to make a computer network that could grow to any size, and be affordable for everyone, and be without a central controller or administration. Governments and corporations may try in vain to gain control, but this is the beauty of the Internet, and why its design is so much better than the original ARPANET, or IBM's SNA contender, or anything else.

When you invent something, people may be incredulous and may not believe it, but in my case just look at my invention and what it has done.

After you have made an invention, keep it as simple as possible, because you will need to prove that it works. When you have convinced everyone, which is the hardest thing to do, they may like what you've invented and put it into use around the world. Then you may also discover that …

It's Cool to be Clever.

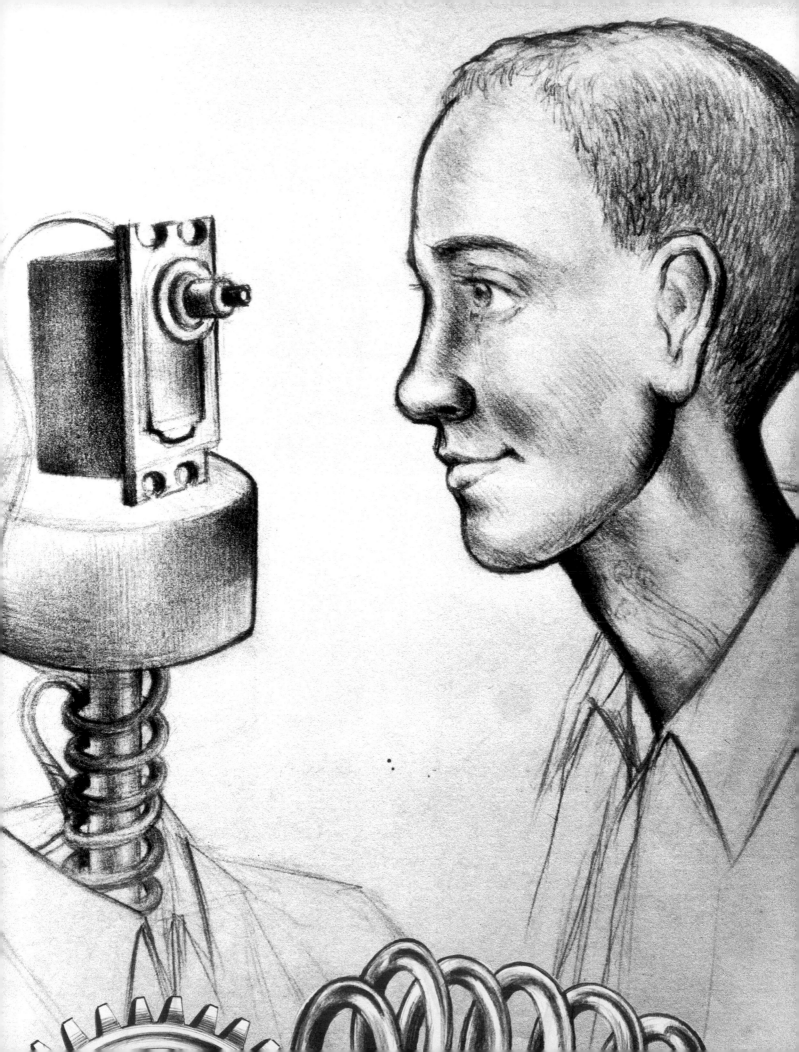

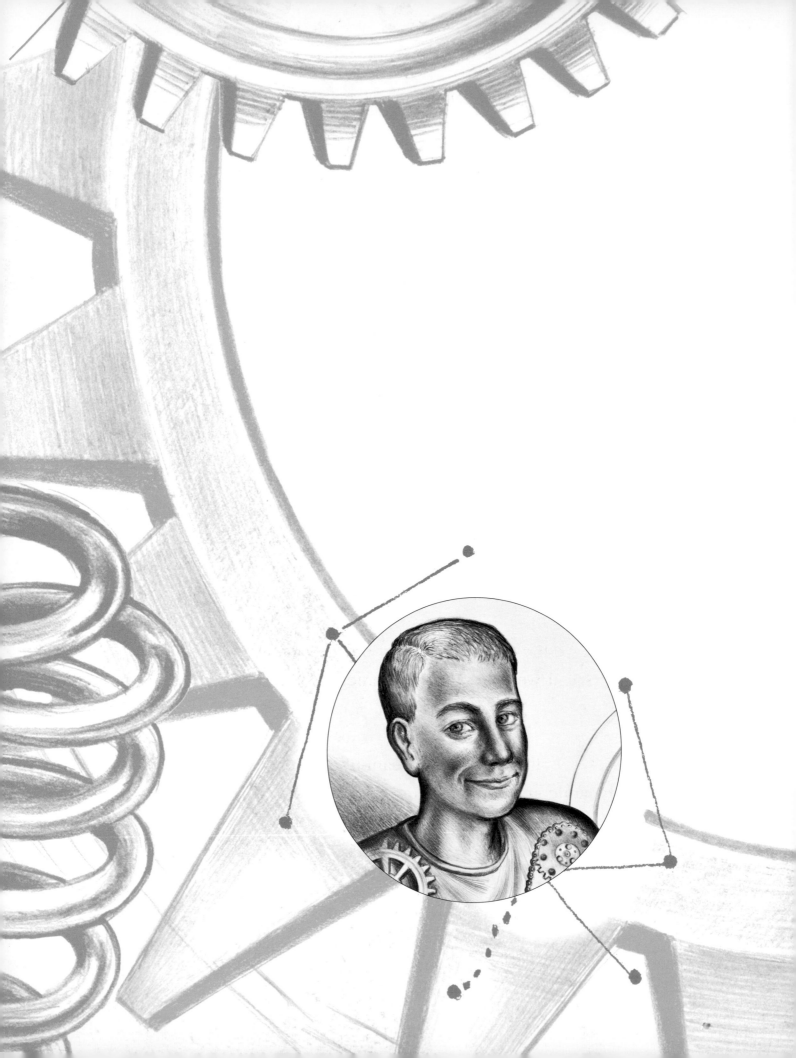

Author **Leanne Jones** is a private investigator living in Victoria, British Columbia, Canada. At one time, when she was a school teacher, she noticed that children of genius need as much encouragement as anyone else. She became interested in Edson Hendricks's story because his ideas led to the greatest invention in the world today. His story is also a story of inspiration for others who have important ideas that should never be lost.

Edson Hendricks left IBM after he couldn't get its management to fully support his VNET design and other research ideas. He joined Linkabit Corporation and later became one of their very earliest employees at ViaSat in Carlsbad, north of San Diego. He now lives in San Diego, where he continues to observe life carefully and try out new ideas. His personal website is www.edh.net.

The pencil drawings of dream-like visions and dynamic gears illuminating the mind of a young inventor were created with magic realism by Victoria illustrator **Anna Mah**.